7 Days to Deeper Intimacy With God

*Awaken your spirit. Align your heart.
Abide in His presence.*

Shana Zolicoffer

Copyright © 2025 by Shana Zolicoffer
All rights reserved.

No part of this publication may be reproduced, stored in a retrieval system, or transmitted in any form or by any means electronic, mechanical, photocopying, recording, or otherwise without the prior written permission of the author, except for brief quotations used in reviews or scholarly articles.

ISBN: 978-1-63960-059-5 (paperback)

Published in the United States by:
Pen2Pad Ink Publishing
www.pen2padink.org | contact@pen2padink.org

Scripture taken from the Holy Bible, New International Version® (NIV®).

Copyright © 1973, 1978, 1984, 2011 by Biblica, Inc.™ Use

.

Table of Contents

Introduction..5

Before You Begin..7

A Word of Encouragement.....................8

The Power of Showing Up on Purpose..............9

Thank You for Letting Me In........................24

Come Close, Come Clean............................37

The Power of Surrender..............................49

Becoming One with the Father......................62

Bow Low Rise Bold..77

Don't Quit Remain Consistent........................92

Other Books by Author Shana Zolicoffer.......107

7 Days to Deeper Intimacy with God

Introduction

Come Closer, God Has Been Waiting for You

A Holy Invitation

Welcome. You didn't stumble across this guide by accident. This is not a coincidence, it's a calling. A sound from Heaven that says, "Come Closer." Before you opened this book, God's eyes were on you. His heart was leaning in towards you, and now, so are you.

This book is a sacred doorway. A divine interruption. A set-apart moment in time where Heaven meets earth, and your soul meets the One who made it. Within these pages, you won't just write words you'll encounter the Word. You won't just pray you'll partner. You won't just reflect, you'll be refined.

Over the next seven days, you will walk through seven foundational pillars that open the door to deeper intimacy with God:

Day 1: Intentionality - The Power of Showing Up on Purpose

Day 2: Gratitude - Thank You for Letting Me In

Day 3: Repentance - Come Clean, Come Close

Day 4: Surrender - The Power of Surrendered Alignment

7 Days to Deeper Intimacy with God

Day 5: Synchronization - Becoming One with the Father

Day 6: Humility - Bow Low. Rise Bold

Day 7: Consistency - Don't Quit Remain Consistent

Each day offers:
- **A Heartfelt Devotion** to center your spirit
- **A Guided Prayer** to help you connect
- **Journal Prompts** to unlock your understanding
- **Declarations** to speak life into your soul
- **A Listening Page** for what God wants to say in return

You don't have to be perfect. You just need to be present. Let go of the pressure to perform. God isn't looking for polished prayers, He's after your posture. You don't need the "right words." All He wants is you.

Before You Begin:
A Reflection Page

Where Am I With God Right Now?

Use this space to honestly assess where you are emotionally, spiritually, and relationally with God. Write without filters. Let this be your starting point.

_____

_____

_____

_____

_____

_____

_____

_____

_____

_____

_____

_____

A Word of Encouragement

This is not a guide for the surface. It's for the seeker. For the hungry. For the one who says, "I want more of You, Lord."

Prayer is not performance. It's a partnership with Heaven.

Intimacy with God isn't earned through perfection; it's birthed through posture, presence, and pursuit.

So come closer. You are welcomed. You are wanted. You are deeply loved.

Let's begin.

With love and expectation,

Shana Zolicoffer

Pastor Shana Zolicoffer
Author, Prophetic Intercessor, Prayer Strategist

Day 1

The Power of Showing Up on Purpose

Scripture

"Draw near to God, and He will draw near to you."
~James 4:8 (ESV)

Devotional

There is something sacred about pursuit. Not the kind that stems from duty or routine, but the kind born from a pure hunger and thirst of the soul to go deeper, to know more, and to be near.

"As the deer pants for streams of water, so my soul pants for you, my God. My soul thirsts for God, for the living God. When can I go and meet with God?

Deep calls to deep in the roar of your waterfalls; all your waves and breakers have swept over me." ~Psalm 42:1-2, 7 (NIV)

This is not surface-level longing. This is the kind of yearning that quiets the noise of the world just to hear the voice of heaven. There's a sacred difference between reciting a quick prayer in passing and choosing to pause intentionally, reverently to sit with the One who shaped time itself. God doesn't force intimacy. He invites it.

And like all real relationships, the depth of that connection is measured by the willingness of both hearts to show up fully. God is always willing. Always present. Always reaching.

The question is...

Are you?

What does it mean to approach God on purpose? It means waking up and choosing Him before the social media scroll or checking your bank account. Declaring His name before the noise of the day begins. Setting aside moments not to perform spiritual duty, but to cultivate divine intimacy. It's silencing distractions, not because they're bad, but because He is greater. This is not about being perfect. It's about being present.

Intentionality means showing up not just with your body, but with your heart and soul. It means saying, "God, I'm here. Not because I want something. Just because I want *You*." When we show up with expectation believing that He is not only listening, but He longs for a response, we position ourselves to experience the fullness of who He is along with transformation.

Too often, we go on autopilot with our prayers. We mumble grace at meals, say "thank You" out of habit, and repeat the same repetitious words every night. But intimacy doesn't just grow through routine, it grows through realness and vulnerability. It's time to awaken your pursuit. Matthew 7:7-8 (NIV) says "Ask, and it will be given to you; seek, and you will find; knock, and the door will be opened to you. For everyone who asks receives; the one who seeks finds; and to the one who knocks, the door will be opened." To become a seeker again you must remember that the King of glory wants to meet with you.

Reposition your life if you must. When you declutter your mind and spirit your frequency will change. Why? Because there is power in pursuit. The blessing is in His presence. Blessed are those who hunger and thirst for righteousness, for they will be filled. Matthew 5:6. God honors hunger. He fills those who make room for Him. So show up on purpose. Not because you have to. But because you *long to*. The nearness you've been craving? It starts with one intentional yes.

Personal Reflection

Pause for a moment and ask yourself

1. Have I been casually seeking God or intentionally prioritizing Him?

_____

_____

_____

_____

2. Am I showing up for God on purpose or out of habit?

_____

_____

_____

_____

3. Have I been more consistent with checking my phone than checking in with my Savior?

_____

_____

_____

_____

4. When was the last time I slowed down just to sit in God's presence with no agenda?

_____

_____

_____

_____

This isn't about shame, it's about invitation. An opportunity to grow closer.

Heart Reflection

Close your eyes. Breathe deeply.
Let your soul speak honestly.

1. Where in your life have you been passive in your pursuit of God?

_____

_____

_____

_____

_____

2. What areas in my life have stolen time from God?

_____

_____

_____

_____

_____

3. What would it look like to rearrange my schedule to reflect that He is my priority?

_____

_____

_____

_____

_____

4. Do I believe God wants to spend time with me? Or have I been approaching Him like a stranger instead of a Father?

_____

_____

_____

_____

_____

Let your heart tell the truth. That's where intimacy begins.

Journal Prompts

Use this space to respond from your heart.

1. What distractions or priorities have taken God's place in my daily life?

_____

_____

_____

_____

2. What would my spiritual life look like if I chose to pursue God on purpose each day?

_____

_____

_____

_____

3. How do I want to feel after spending time with God? What am I truly longing for?

_____

_____

_____

_____

_____

4. Write down 3 specific ways you will intentionally make room for God today.

_____

_____

_____

_____

_____

5. "What does choosing God look like for me today?"

_____

_____

_____

7 Days to Deeper Intimacy with God

_____

_____

_____

_____

_____

_____

_____

_____

_____

_____

_____

_____

_____

_____

_____

_____

Write freely. Let the pen become your prayer.

Guided Prayer:
A Prayer of Intentional Pursuit

Father,

I'm here. Not because I want something from You, but because I want more of You. Forgive me for the times I've come to You out of habit or routine. Today, I choose to seek You on purpose. Teach me how to sit with You, to listen for Your voice, and to love Your presence more than I love anything else. Rearrange what needs to be rearranged in my life so that You're at the center again. I don't want a surface connection. I want deep communion. Meet me here.

In Jesus' name,

Amen

Prayer Prompt

Write your own simple prayer from the heart.

Lord Jesus,

I admit I've let some things get in the way of our time together. But today, I make space for you. I choose to come closer not because I'm perfect, but because I know You're worth it. Help me prioritize You in my everyday life. Help me long for You again. _____ (continue writing...)

_____

_____

_____

_____

_____

_____

_____

_____

_____

Daily Declaration

I will seek God on purpose.
I choose intimacy over
busyness. His presence
is my priority. He doesn't
have to chase me,
I'm chasing Him.
I am drawn to God,
and He is drawn to me.

**Speak it boldly. Every word
is a seed of pursuit.**

Listening Moment

Now that you've journaled, prayed, and declared, take a few moments in silence.

Prompt: God, what are You inviting me into today? What do You want me to be intentional about in this season?

_____

_____

_____

_____

_____

_____

_____

_____

Close your eyes. Listen. Write down any words, pictures, Scriptures, or quiet impressions you sense. Don't overthink it, just receive.

Shana Zolicoffer

When the Spirit of God Speaks

Day 2

Thank You for Letting Me In

Scripture

"Enter His gates with thanksgiving, and His courts with praise! Give thanks to Him; bless His name!"
~Psalm 100:4 (ESV)

Devotional

Gratitude is the doorway to revelation where your eyes open, your heart softens, and you realize just how powerful this moment truly is. Have you ever stepped into a room that felt too grand for your past? A space so sacred, you silently wondered, "Am I even supposed to be here?" You held your breath, bracing for rejection. But instead of shame slamming the door, God flung it wide open and said, "Welcome in."

Gratitude rises when you realize this access wasn't earned, it was gifted. You didn't earn this seat at the table. You didn't deserve this kind of love. You didn't fight your way into God's presence. He *let* you in. Not because of your perfection, but because of His promise. His faithfulness. His unfailing mercy. It cost Him everything and He still said *yes* to you.

Gratitude is the song of a heart that remembers. It remembers the pit He pulled you from, the prayers He answered in silence, the grace that never ran out. It bows low not out of guilt, but out of awe. And with trembling lips it says, "Thank You for choosing me when You had every reason not to."

Yes, it's easy to ask for more; more peace, more favor, more provision. But today we shift the posture of our hearts to thank Him not just for what He's done, but for who He is. The Almighty One.

We thank Him for being Sovereign, for being our Strong Tower, our Great Defender when everything else was falling apart. We thank Him for covering us in righteousness when shame tried to undress us. For pulling us close when fear told us to stay away. For calling us His own, not reluctantly, but delightedly.

Gratitude changes everything. It humbles you. It heals you. And it opens your eyes to see just how deeply loved you really are. You didn't sneak into grace. You were invited.

So pause. Breathe. And say it loud enough for heaven to hear:

"Thank You."

Personal Reflection

Pause for a moment to reflect on how God has responded to you during these 7 days then ask yourself

1. When was the last time I thanked God just for letting me be near Him?

_____

_____

_____

_____

2. What areas of my life reflect His grace that I often overlook?

_____

_____

_____

_____

Heart Reflection

Lord God,

I don't want to rush past Your kindness. Help me slow down and truly feel the weight of Your precence. Let my heart overflow with thanksgiving not just for the gifts, but for the Giver that you are.

In Jesus Name,

Amen

Journal Prompt

Use this space to respond from your heart.

1. What have I learned about God in these 7 days?

_____

_____

_____

_____

2. What has shifted in my heart?

_____

_____

_____

_____

3. Write a thank-you letter to God today. Don't ask for anything.

_____

_____

_____

_____

_____

4. Just thank Him for letting you into His family, His presence, His plans.

_____

_____

_____

_____

_____

Gratitude List

Write 10 things you're grateful for in your walk with God, past, present, or future.

1._____

_____

2._____

_____

3._____

_____

4._____

_____

5._____

_____

6._____

_____

Shana Zolicoffer

7._____

_____

8._____

_____

9._____

_____

10._____

_____

Guided Prayer of Thankfulness:
A Prayer of Gratitude

Father,

You are the Giver of every good thing. You didn't have to meet me here, but You graciously did. Thank You for letting me in. You didn't owe me access. Not reluctantly, but lovingly. Not because I earned it, but because grace made room. Thank You for seeing past my faults, for loving me through my shame, and choosing to dwell with me anyway. You didn't just tolerate me You embraced me and You desired me. You tore the veil so I could come close.

Today, I sit in awe. Not because I've done everything right, but because You've never stopped being God. Let every breath I breathe be filled with thanks. Let my worship be rooted in wonder. Let every beat of my heart echo: *Thank You, Father.* For every unseen mercy, for every undeserved invitation, for every moment You drew close when I didn't know I needed You I say thank You. You didn't have to let me in but You did. And I will never take that for granted.

In Jesus' name,

Amen

Prayer Prompt

List 5 things God has already done for you that you may have taken for granted. Thank Him out loud for each one.

1._____

_____

2._____

_____

3._____

_____

4._____

_____

5._____

_____

Daily Declaration

I don't need permission God has already given me access. I walk through His open doors with gratitude, not guilt. I belong here, not because of me, but because of Him.

Listening Moment

Take 3–5 minutes in silence.

Ask: God, what gift do You want me to carry forward from this experience? What do You want me to thank You for today that I may have overlooked?

_____

_____

_____

_____

_____

_____

_____

_____

_____

_____

Write down what comes to your heart even the small, quiet blessings.

When the Spirit of God Speaks

Day 3

Come Clean, Come Close

Scripture

"Create in me a clean heart, O God, and renew a right spirit within me." ~Psalm 51:10 (ESV)

Devotional

Repentance is not God turning His face in disappointment, it's Him opening His arms, saying "Turn and Come back home."

Somewhere along the journey, many of us learned to associate repentance with punishment. We were taught to brace ourselves for guilt, shame, and disqualification. But the truth is, repentance was never about exile, it's a beautiful reunion, an invitation to step out of sin into the mercies of His love and compassion.

Repentance is not punishment, it's God's loving permission to be open, honest, to repent and to start again. "Therefore, since we are surrounded by such a huge crowd of witnesses to the life of faith, let us strip off every weight that slows us down, especially the sin that so easily trips us up.

And let us run with endurance the race God has set before us." Hebrews 12:1 (NLT)

David wasn't just begging for forgiveness in Psalm 51 he was reaching for restoration. He wasn't merely seeking a clean slate; he was desperate for closeness. His cry wasn't rooted in fear of punishment; it was fueled by a deep longing. "Do not cast me away from Your presence. Don't take Your Holy Spirit from me." David didn't fear God's wrath as much as he feared His absence. He wanted the nearness of God more than he wanted relief from guilt. This is what true repentance looks like. It's not about rehearsing shame; it's about reclaiming intimacy.

Repentance doesn't condemn you; it clears the path to connection. It removes the heavy layers of sin, silence, and shame that try to choke the voice of your spirit. It breaks the stillness between your heart and heaven. It reminds you that you are *not* disqualified by your mistakes.

"There is therefore now no condemnation to those who are in Christ Jesus, who walk not after the flesh, but after the Spirit." ~Romans 8:1 (KJV)

God isn't turned off by your truth He's drawn to it. He doesn't flinch at your failure; He leans into it. So let it out. The broken pieces. The ugly parts. The things you thought disqualified you. They are not too much for God. You are not too far gone. You are not too broken to be restored.

Every time you choose repentance, you're

choosing relationship over regret. You're choosing presence over performance. And the moment you take one step toward Him He runs the rest of the way toward you.

Don't shrink back. Come closer.

Personal Reflection

Take a moment to pause.
Breathe deeply. Ask yourself:

1. What have you been carrying that's been weighing on your spirit?

_____

_____

_____

_____

_____

2. What do you know you need to release, confess, or bring into the light?

_____

_____

_____

_____

_____

There is no condemnation here, only compassion. This is your safe space to be honest and to be healed.

Heart Reflection

Lord Jesus,

I've tried to manage my own mess, patch my own heart, and hide my flaws. But I'm tired. I want You more than I want to be right. I need You more than I need to appear strong. Cleanse my heart. Quiet my fears. Heal my hidden places. I repent. I return. I rest in You.

In Jesus' name,

Amen

Journal Prompts

Use this space to respond from your heart.

1. What area(s) of my life do I need to bring into the light?

_____

_____

_____

_____

_____

2. Have I confused repentance with shame in the past?

_____

_____

_____

_____

_____

3. How would it feel to fully embrace God's mercy for me today?

_____

_____

_____

_____

_____

4. What do I believe God wants to restore in me?

_____

_____

_____

_____

Guided Prayer:
A Prayer of Forgiveness

Lord God,

Thank You for being a safe place for my truth. I come to You without a mask, without excuses, and without fear. I repent for anything that has taken Your place in my heart. Forgive me. Cleanse me. Renew me. Restore me. Let nothing come between us to separate us. I'm Yours again, Thank You for accepting me and loving me back to life.

In Jesus' name,

Amen

Prayer Prompt

Write your own simple prayer from the heart.

Lord, what is one thing You want me to release today so I can grow closer to You?

_____

_____

_____

_____

_____

_____

_____

_____

_____

Sit with this question in stillness and let the Holy Spirit reveal what's ready to be surrendered.

Daily Declaration

I am not condemned. I am forgiven, I am cleansed, I am chosen, and I am cherished. Repentance is my doorway to deeper love. God is not distant. He is drawing me closer with every surrendered breath.

Listening Moment

God, what would You like to say to me now?

_____

_____

_____

_____

_____

_____

_____

_____

_____

_____

Leave this space blank in your book or journal for the reader to write what they hear in their spirit. Some may draw, some may write, some may simply sit and listen. But God always responds to a heart that returns to Him.

When the Spirit of God Speaks

Day 4

The Power of Surrendered Alignment

Scripture

"Not my will, but Yours be done." ~ Luke 22:42

Devotional

Posture is far more than the position of your body; it's the position of your soul. It's not just bowed knees or lifted hands; it's the silent surrender of your heart. It's the inner alignment that says, "Even when it costs me everything, I choose You." True submission is not weakness. It's a sacred strength that defies the logic of flesh. It's the moment when your will is screaming to run, to fix it, to hold on and you choose instead to yield. To bow low. To softly speak in trembling faith, "Not my will, but Yours be done."

This is the posture of the Spirit. The posture of Jesus in the garden of Gethsemane. In the thick of sorrow, under the weight of what was to come, He didn't resist the will of the Father. He denied His flesh. He yielded His fear. He surrendered His comfort. And in doing so, He modeled the kind of holy alignment that births glory.

John 17:21-23 captures the longing of Jesus' heart: "I pray that they will all be one, just as you and I are one as you are in me, Father, and I am in you... May they experience such perfect unity that the world will know that you sent me and that you love them as much as you love me."

This is not surface-level unity. This is divine synchronization. To become one with God is to willingly crucify the flesh so that the Spirit can reign. It's to allow the will of the Father to override your feelings, your fears, your need for control. This kind of unity is born in the furnace of submission not just doing His will, but becoming His will.

To posture yourself before God is to say, "Even if it hurts, even if it stretches me, even if it strips me of everything I thought I needed I trust You more than I trust me." And it's in that place where flesh is denied and faith rises up that transformation happens. In surrender, you are not diminished; you are refined. You are not losing control; you are gaining access. You are not bowing out; you are being lifted into divine purpose.

So today, posture your heart. Open your hands. Loosen your grip. And step into divine alignment with the One who knows the way, sees the end, and loves you enough to carry you through it. Because in the surrender, there is glory. In the obedience, there is breakthrough. And in the posture of your heart, He finds a place to dwell.

Personal Reflection

Take a moment to pause. Breathe deeply. Ask yourself:

1. Have I truly given God access to every area of my life?

_____

_____

_____

_____

2. Do I trust Him enough to submit even when I don't understand?

_____

_____

_____

_____

Sometimes, our mouths say, *"Your will be done,"* but our hearts whisper, *"as long as I agree."* Let today be the day you wrestle that part of yourself into submission and reverence, not through pressure, but through love.

Heart Reflection

Use this space to respond from your heart.

1. Where do you feel tension when God asks you to let go?

_____

_____

_____

_____

_____

2. What are you gripping that God may be gently asking you to release?

_____

_____

_____

_____

_____

3. Is there a specific area, your time, a relationship, your future that you're guarding from His touch?

_____

_____

_____

_____

_____

Let your heart speak honestly here. He already knows, and He is not intimidated by your wrestling. He meets you in it.

Journal Prompt:

Use this space to respond from your heart.

1. What areas of my life am I still trying to control?

_____

_____

_____

_____

_____

2. How can I physically and spiritually posture myself in reverence today?

_____

_____

_____

_____

_____

3. What would full submission look like in this season of my life?

_____

_____

_____

_____

4. What does submission truly feel like in my spirit? Where do I resist it most, and why?

_____

_____

_____

_____

5. In what areas of my life am I trying to maintain control instead of trusting God's plan?

_____

_____

6. How can I physically or symbolically express my surrender to God today (e.g., open hands, kneeling, writing it down)?

Write with vulnerability. Let your journal become an altar.

Guided Prayer of Submission

Dear Lord,

Break what must be broken in me so that I may be fully Yours. I surrender my need to always understand, my desire to always lead, and the fears that keep me from letting go. Let my heart kneel before You not just in moments of crisis, but in daily trust. Teach me the beauty of submission, and let my posture reflect my surrender.

In Jesus' name,

Amen

Prayer Prompt

Lord Jesus,

Today I choose to bow before you not my knees, but my will, my pride, my agenda. I've tried to carry and control things You never asked me to. Help me trust that what You want *for* me is far greater than what I want *from* You. _____ (write your own continuation…)

_____

_____

_____

_____

_____

_____

_____

_____

_____

Daily Declaration

My soul submits.
My heart obeys.
I find strength in surrender.

Say this aloud. Speak it until your soul believes it. God hears you and He's proud of your yes.

Listening Moment

Be still. Open your heart and write what you sense God is speaking to you.

Prompt: Father, what part of me are You asking for today?

_____

_____

_____

_____

_____

_____

_____

_____

_____

Write down any thoughts, images, or Scriptures that come to mind. Don't filter just receive.

Shana Zolicoffer

When the Spirit of God Speaks

Day 5

Becoming One with the Father

Scripture

"Abide in Me, and I in you." – John 15:4

Devotional

There is a divine rhythm to the heart of God, a sacred cadence not meant to be observed from a distance, but to be lived in. It is the rhythm of intimacy, of oneness, of dwelling so deeply in Him that your steps echo His will. It's not just about knowing God from afar, it's about becoming one with Him emerging your will, your desires, your thoughts, and your actions with the flow of His Spirit.

To synchronize with God is to align your entire being body, mind, and spirit with His divine will. It's not a one-time moment, but a lifestyle. A posture. A continual yielding of your flesh, your fears, your timelines, and your ambitions to the sovereignty of a Father who sees far beyond what you can imagine. This alignment is not a performance. It's a partnership, an invitation into spiritual maturity, where transformation is birthed in the soil of surrender.

Jesus modeled this sacred sync perfectly. He didn't move in haste. He didn't strive. He didn't act out of pressure or panic. His every move flowed from alignment with the Father. "I only do what I see My Father doing," He said. That's not just discipline; that's divine harmony. That's spiritual intimacy, that is relationship. That's the blueprint.

But how often do we find ourselves out of the flow of God? Rushing ahead, trying to fix what only God can heal. Lagging behind, paralyzed by doubt, fatigue, or fear. Working for God while disconnected from Him. Trying to manifest purpose without abiding in presence. We grow weary because we're moving outside the will of God. We're striving instead of surrendering.

But God isn't looking for your perfection. He's after your heart posture. He's calling you to settle your soul into the unity of His Spirit to stay, dwell, and abide in Him until you begin to move as one. To trust His Spirit so deeply that your yes becomes immediate. Your obedience becomes a joy, not a chore. Your peace becomes immeasurable - limitless because it's no longer tied to outcomes, but to Purpose.

This kind of alignment unlocks something supernatural. When you stay in sync with the Father, you begin to evolve. Growth is no longer forced, it's organic. Revelation comes without striving. Wisdom flows without panic. Miracles manifest not from manipulation, but from alignment. You begin to live not just for God but from God. He becomes your source, your strategy, your sustainer.

So today, pause. Realign. Not just in word, but in deed. Let your mind be renewed. Let your steps be recalibrated. Let your soul come back into unity with the Father. Deny your flesh the right to lead, and yield instead to the gentle guidance of the Spirit.

Because there is no greater intimacy than moving in sync with the One who made you. When your heart beats with His earnest, steady, surrender you won't have to chase destiny. You'll *become* it. And in that place, you'll find His Peace. Purpose. Power and Presence that you were made to dwell in forever.

Personal Reflection

Ask yourself today

1. Have I been moving ahead of God, trying to make things happen in my own strength?

_____

_____

_____

_____

_____

2. Am I dragging behind because of fear, doubt, or exhaustion?

_____

_____

_____

_____

_____

3. What would change if I fully trusted God's pace?

_____

_____

_____

_____

_____

Let your answers lead you back to alignment.

Heart Reflection

Close your eyes. Picture yourself walking with God.

1. What's the current state of my life: rushed, disconnected, or frantic?

_____

_____

_____

_____

_____

2. What is God compassionately asking me to slow down or surrender so I can move with Him?

_____

_____

_____

_____

3. What part of my life feels out of alignment with His heart right now?

_____

_____

_____

_____

_____

Let the Holy Spirit guide your awareness, not into guilt but into grace-filled alignment.

Journal Prompt

Use this space to respond from your heart

1. Have I been moving ahead of God, behind Him, or beside Him?

_____

_____

_____

_____

_____

2. Have I been more focused on doing *for* God rather than *being* with Him?

_____

_____

_____

_____

_____

3. What does synchronization with God look like in my relationships, goals, and decisions?

_____

_____

_____

_____

_____

4. What areas in my life do I need to return to God's rhythm?

_____

_____

_____

_____

_____

5. What does spiritual alignment look like for me now?

_____

_____

_____

_____

_____

Let it flow freely. Write without revising yourself. Allow this page to hold your truth and your turning point.

Guided Prayer:
A Prayer for Synchronization

Lord God,

I'm tired of rushing ahead of You. I'm weary of lagging behind. I want to walk with You not just in moments of worship, but in the way I live, think, decide, and move. Teach me Your rhythm so that my rhythms will be able to reflect Your heart as I move. Slow me down where I've been hurried. Wake me up where I've grown numb. I want Your timing. I want Your guidance and you leading me. Let my heart beat in harmony with Yours.

In Jesus' name,

Amen

Prayer Prompt

Lord God,

I surrender the parts of my life that have been moving without You. I give You my pace, my plans, and my pressure. Lead me into alignment. Don't let me miss what You're doing because I'm too focused on what I want. Teach me to abide. _____ (continue your personal prayer...)

_____

_____

_____

_____

_____

_____

_____

_____

Daily Declaration

I move in sync with the
Spirit. I walk with God,
not ahead of Him
or behind.

Say it with faith.
Feel it in your spirit.
Let it become your
new rhythm.

Listening Moment

Find stillness. Let the silence create space for God's voice.

Prompt: God, what do You want to do *with* me today?

_____

_____

_____

_____

_____

_____

_____

_____

_____

Listen. You may sense a word, a nudge, or a subtle invitation. Allow the Holy Spirit to speak. Write down whatever rises in your spirit.

When the Spirit of God Speaks

Day 6

Bow Low. Rise Bold

Scriptures

"God resists the proud, but gives grace to the humble." ~James 4:6

"Let us come boldly to the throne of grace." ~Hebrews 4:16

Devotional

True intimacy with God is not performance, it's posture. It's the sacred space where your trembling meets your trusting, your ache collides with your assurance, and your weakness becomes a platform for His strength. You don't have to choose between being bold and being humble because in the Kingdom, these two are not opposites, they are divine companions.

The world will tell you humility is shrinking, hiding, or playing small. But that's not Heaven's definition. Shrinking says, *"I'm not worthy to be seen."* But humility says, *"God, I trust You to do what I cannot."* One is rooted in fear, the other in faith. And when you walk in Kingdom humility, you walk knowing everything you have, every gift, every open door, every breath is because of Him. It is the deep acknowledgment that "every good and perfect gift comes from above" (James 1:17), and that "apart from Him, we can do nothing" (John 15:5).

Humility grounds us. It keeps our hearts soft, surrendered, and in sync with the Father. It quiets pride and postures us to receive grace. "God resists the proud, but gives grace to the humble" (James 4:6). He lifts those who bow low not because of what they can do, but because they know where their help comes from.

And confidence? It isn't arrogance. It isn't self-made or ego-driven. Confidence in God is born from encountering His faithfulness. It's the holy boldness that rises not in your own ability, but in the unshakable assurance that *"He who began a good work in you will carry it on to completion until the day of Christ Jesus"* (Philippians 1:6). You can *rest* and *occupy* what's to come not because you're fearless, but because your faith is anchored in the One who finishes what He starts.

Sometimes, we don't lack faith, we just need more confidence in the God we already trust. Like the father in Mark 9:24, we cry, *"Lord, I believe; help my unbelief."* That cry is holy. That vulnerability is worship. And in that tension between what you know and what you're still learning to trust, God meets you. Not with shame, but with strength. Not with distance, but with deepening presence.

When you align yourself with God your thoughts, your desires, your decisions, even the rhythm of your breath you become in tune with His Spirit. You no longer move by impulse or fear, but by divine orchestration. His will becomes your compass, His voice your guide, and His presence your anchor.

In that sacred space of full surrender and holy synchronization, transformation takes root. You begin to shed the weight of who you were and rise into the truth of who you were always created to be. The more you yield, the more you evolve not by striving, but by abiding. Not by forcing, but by flowing.

This alignment doesn't erase you; it unveils you. It doesn't make you less, it makes you whole. You become refined in the fire of obedience. Strengthened in the stillness of trust and awakened to your divine identity. You are not just walking with God, you are becoming like Him. And in that becoming, the miraculous unfolds.

Humility keeps you grounded in God's grace. Confidence lifts your eyes to what's possible in Him. And together, they unlock doors that striving never could.

So yes bow low. Let your knees hit the floor. Acknowledge your need for Him. But don't stay there in shame. Rise bold. Walk in the identity

He's already secured for you. Trust the Spirit who dwells in you, leads you, and aligns you with the Father's heart.

You don't have to perform to be loved. You don't have to have it all together to be chosen. The cross already settled that. You are not just tolerated in His presence. You are welcomed, wanted, and compassionately loved.

So bring it all, your faith and your fear. Your questions and your confidence. Your surrender and your strength.

Because when Heaven sees humility, it leans in. And when Hell sees confidence in Christ, it trembles.

Personal Reflection

The beauty of being fully known and still fully loved. Ask yourself honestly.

1. Have I been trying to earn God's presence or prove myself worthy?

_____

_____

_____

_____

_____

2. Do I come to God timidly, unsure if He truly wants to hear from me?

_____

_____

_____

_____

_____

3. Where have I confused false humility with fear or self-doubt?

_____

_____

_____

_____

_____

This is your safe space to untangle those feelings and bring them to the Light.

Heart Reflection

Let your soul speak freely

1. What part of me struggles to kneel, to surrender, to admit weakness?

_____

_____

_____

_____

2. What part of me struggles to rise to believe I'm enough, loved, and empowered?

_____

_____

_____

_____

3. Have I truly accepted that I am both small before God and secure in Him?

_____
_____
_____
_____
_____

Write without shame. Let grace speak louder than guilt.

Journal Prompts

Use this space to respond from your heart

1. What would it look like for me to live from a place of *humble confidence*?

_____

_____

_____

_____

_____

2. Where have I been hiding in shame instead of coming boldly?

_____

_____

_____

_____

_____

3. Where do I need to kneel again? Where do I need to rise again?

_____
_____
_____
_____
_____

4. How does God want to redefine my view of confidence today?

_____
_____
_____
_____
_____

Capture your thoughts, your prayers, and any healing truths that emerge.

Guided Prayer:
A Prayer of Bold Humility

Lord God,

I come to you today as imperfect as I am not in fear, but in faith. I lay down my pride, my need to impress, and my hidden shame. I know You're not asking me to have it all together You're just asking me to come. So, I come to you bringing my brokenness and my belief. I kneel low, but I rise bold because You said I could. Thank You for welcoming me. Thank You for calling me Yours.

In Jesus' name,

Amen

Prayer Prompt

Lord God,

Sometimes I doubt I belong in Your presence. Sometimes I act like I have to clean myself up before I come close. But today, I surrender that lie. I choose to approach You just as I am humbled, but hopeful. Let Your grace carry me... _____ (continue your prayer)

Daily Declaration

I am humble before God and confident in His love. I am humbly confident. God delights in my presence. He welcomes me here.

Declare it aloud. Let your voice shake if it has to but let your soul stand strong

Listening Moment

Still your heart. Breathe deep.
Let the noise fall away.

Prompt: Lord, what truth do You want me to believe about myself today?

_____

_____

_____

_____

_____

_____

_____

_____

_____

Listen for His voice. It may come as a word, an inner knowing, a Scripture, or a name He's given you. Write down whatever He places on your heart without filtering or doubting.

Shana Zolicoffer

When the Spirit of God Speaks

Day 7

Don't Quit Remain Consistent

Scripture

"Let us not grow weary in doing good, for at the proper time we will reap a harvest if we do not give up." ~Galatians 6:9 (NIV)

"Therefore, my dear brothers and sisters, stand firm. Let nothing move you. Always give yourselves fully to the work of the Lord, because you know that your labor in the Lord is not in vain." ~1 Corinthians 15:58 (NIV)

Devotional

Consistency is more than a habit. It's a solidary gesture, an act of spiritual defiance against discouragement, doubt, and delay. It's choosing to show up even when the results don't. It's waking up each day telling God "yes" again and again, even when the fire has faded and the finish line feels far away.

The Word tells us, *"The race is not given to the swift or to the strong, but to the one who endures to the end"* (Ecclesiastes 9:11, paraphrased). This race we're running isn't about speed or spotlight, it's about endurance. It's about pressing forward when everything in you wants to give up. It's about persevering through the silence, the noise, the setbacks, and the seasons that seem barren.

James 1:4 (ESV) says, "And let steadfastness have its full effect, that you may be perfect and complete, lacking in nothing." In other words, let consistency have its way in you. Believing that when you keep showing up, when you stay faithful in the tedious, the miraculous is being established beneath the surface.

Consistency often breaks resistance and limitations. It silences the lies that tell you it's not worth it. It shatters mental, emotional and spiritual barriers and makes room for supernatural growth. Every single time you refuse to quit, momentum builds. Heaven arises and legacy is being birthed.

Hebrews 12:3 (NLT) urges us, "Think of all the hostility He endured from sinful people; then you won't become weary and give up." Jesus modeled consistency even unto death. His steady "yes" to the Father wasn't always easy, but it was always unwavering. And now He invites us to do the same.

There will be days when you feel depleted. The prayers you've prayed seem to bounce off the ceiling or go unanswered. Your passion will sometimes feel diminished. Days when it seems like the heavens are silent, the answers delayed, and your passion has grown dim under the weight of disappointment and weariness. You begin to wonder: *Is He listening? Does He still care?* But in those very moments when everything in you wants to retreat its prayer that becomes your lifeline.

Luke 18:1 tells us, "Then Jesus told His disciples a parable to show them that they should always pray and not give up." These were not casual words. This was an urgent charge, a divine reminder that prayer is not just for the good days, but for the hard ones the days you feel dry, discouraged, or defeated.

Consistent prayer is not just a routine, it's a weapon. It anchors your spirit when everything around you is shifting. It keeps your soul intertwined with truth when your emotions are unstable. It creates a continual connection with Heaven, a spiritual lifeline that doesn't rely on your feelings, but on your faith.

Even when you don't have the words, your groanings are heard (Romans 8:26). When your strength is faint, prayer becomes your surrender. It is in these unseen, uncelebrated moments of faithful, tear-stained persistence that some of the greatest breakthroughs begin to form.

Persistent prayer is an act of war against spiritual stagnation. It aligns your heart with the will of God. It keeps Heaven's frequency open over your life, even when all seems quiet. So keep praying not just when it's easy, but especially when it's hard. Because every declared "Amen," every faith-filled sigh, every moment you choose to persevere instead of giving up, He sees it. And He honors it.

Don't underestimate the power of your sacrifice. It's not just about the mountaintop moments, it's the hard challenges, the faithful steps that build eternal inheritance. You're not just praying into thin air. You're building a track record, a history with God. And on the other side of your persistence is promise. Every time you pray in the dark, every time you serve when you're tired, every time you believe when it hurts, you're sowing into something divine. That is strength. That is resilience. That is worship. Your consistent pursuit is never wasted. God sees. God hears. God remembers. God rewards. God is working behind the scenes of your YES. Heaven is watching. Heaven is cheering. Heaven is backing you.

So don't quit. Stay anchored. Heaven is still moving!

Personal Reflection

Use this space to respond from your heart.

1. Where have I been tempted to give up because I haven't seen results?

_____

_____

_____

_____

_____

2. What does "faithful in the little" look like for me right now?

_____

_____

_____

_____

_____

Heart Reflection

Lord,

Remind me that showing up matters even when no one sees but You. Help me trust that You are working behind the scenes as I stay the course.

In Jesus' name,

Amen

Journal Prompt

Use this space to respond from your heart.

Write about an area in your life where you've stayed consistent, even when it was hard.

_____

_____

_____

_____

_____

_____

_____

_____

_____

How has God met you in that place? How do you want to keep going from here?

Guided Prayer:
A Prayer for Endurance

Lord God,

I'm tired. Some days feel harder than others to remain consistent. But I know You haven't called me to perfection You've called me to faithfulness. Help me to keep preservering and showing up. When I feel uncertain, remind me that You notice every step. When I feel unqualified, remind me that You called me to this place. When I feel weary, remind me that my harvest is coming. I trust You, even when I don't see the fruit yet. I will not quit, not because I'm strong, but because You are.

In Jesus' name,

Amen

Prayer Prompt

Ask God to reveal one area where He wants you to keep going without rushing or quitting.

Pray for the grace and the strength to uphold the things that require my consistency.

Daily Declaration

I will remain steadfast even when I don't see the results. Because I know Heaven sees the seeds.

My consistency is my offering, my sacrifice is my worship, my obedience is my reward.

I won't give up because my faith isn't rooted in outcomes, it's rooted in Him.

Heaven will water what I've sown, and in due season, it will reap the harvest.

Listening Moment

Sit with God in silence for 3–5 minutes.

Ask: God, how are You inviting me to trust You again? God, what fruit is growing from the seeds I've sown in faith?

_____

_____

_____

_____

_____

_____

_____

_____

_____

Let His Spirit remind you of the ways your sacrifices have not been wasted.

Shana Zolicoffer

When the Spirit of God Speaks

When the Spirit of God Speaks

When the Spirit of God Speaks

When the Spirit of God Speaks

Other Books by Author Shana Zolicoffer

Be sure to follow on social media

 @ShanaZolicoffer

www.ingramcontent.com/pod-product-compliance
Lightning Source LLC
Chambersburg PA
CBHW061739070526
44585CB00024B/2735